AMERSHAM AT WORK

PEOPLE AND INDUSTRIES THROUGH THE YEARS

WILLIAM PARKER

AMBERLEY

First published 2017

Amberley Publishing
The Hill, Stroud
Gloucestershire, GL5 4EP

www.amberley-books.com

ISBN 978 1 4456 7482 7 (print)
ISBN 978 1 4456 7483 4 (ebook)

British Library Cataloguing in Publication Data.
A catalogue record for this book is available
from the British Library.

Origination by Amberley Publishing.
Printed in the UK.

CONTENTS

A TALE OF TWO TOWNS

For 1,000 years Amersham was a single town that grew up on the ancient road from Aylesbury to London where the Misbourne Valley is at its narrowest point, and where in the eighteenth century the turnpike road from Hatfield to Reading crossed at a bridge over the River Misbourne. North of the town, overlooking the beech woods and fields of the Misbourne Valley, lay the farming hamlet of Amersham Common. Here, in the nineteenth century, spawned by the arrival of the Metropolitan Railway, the new town of Amersham-on-the-Hill sprang up. Today the Old Town remains one of the most unspoilt Buckinghamshire towns. Signs of its early industries are everywhere: in the market place, on the High Street, on the site of the brewery beside St Mary's Church, along the Broadway and further east at Bury End. But for Amersham the arrival of the railway changed everything. A dormitory town spread out from the new railway station on the hill and a roll call of successful, modern businesses and industries made Amersham-on-the-Hill and its surrounding area their home. To the east, the new Metro-land Amersham spilled down the hill to join the Old Town, but this separation of historic Amersham and its offspring on the hill both preserved the charm and beauty of the old town and allowed the new town to lead the way in modern suburban development and industrial progress, largely uninhibited by concern for conservation. In this way the flag of industrial progress was carried up the hill and planted firmly on the old common grazing lands between Chesham Bois and Loudhams Farm, which eventually became the village of Little Chalfont.

So the story of *Amersham at Work* is the story of two towns: Old Amersham and Amersham-on-the-Hill. The aim of this book is to chart the origins, growth and in some instances the demise of industries, businesses and institutions that thrived within or just beyond living memory. It is said that one of the advantages of a market economy is that it destroys the companies that fall behind with outdated products and ideas but allows new enterprise to spring up on the ruins of the old. When we look at a modern retail phenomenon, like the Tesco superstore at Bury End on the edge of the Old Town, we are actually looking at the site of an eighteenth-century cotton mill (traces of the mill race can still be seen behind the supermarket), also the site of a one-time national supplier of pies and sausages. So while this account of working Amersham concentrates on the pre- and post-Second World War period, it also looks at the businesses that laid the foundations on which industry in modern Amersham was built.

The book looks at how work changed in four specific locations: in the heart of the Old Town, at Bury End, around the railway station on the hill, and east of Amersham-on-the-Hill along the Watford Road.

Of course industry permeates every corner of this ancient and modern town. Moreover, the concept of Metro-land itself means that thousands of Amersham residents leave the town each day to work in London and places as far afield as Oxford, Reading, Slough, Watford, Aylesbury and Milton Keynes.

The wide variety of work, the ability to embrace the new while preserving the old, the marriage of countryside and commerce, and the sheer convenience of the town is what makes Amersham the prosperous place it is today. A study of working life might seem an odd perspective to take on the life of a town and yet it is work that makes the world go round. And nowhere is that more true than in the beautiful Buckinghamshire town of Amersham.

William Parker, 2017

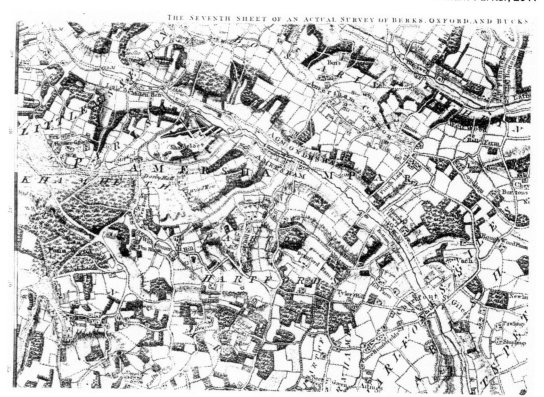

A map of Amersham and the surrounding area drawn around 1760.

AMERSHAM OLD TOWN

WORK IN DAYS GONE BY

Imagine we are standing on the corner of Market Square and The Broadway in Old Amersham 250 years ago. Looking in one direction we can see St Mary's Church and the small stone bridge over the River Misbourne. In front of us is the Market Hall with its open ground floor and council meeting room above. Beyond the Market Hall the wide high street is full of sheep driven in from neighbouring farms. Creaking horse-drawn carts laden with sacks of wheat thread their way through the town to the mill beside the river on the eastern side of the town. Amidst the throng, carts deliver beech wood chairs for onward carriage to London. Farmers trade animal hides with tanners, who ply their trade with the town's shoemakers, glovers, britches makers, saddlers and harness makers. The smell of horse manure fills the air. There is the din of hammers and mallets at blacksmiths and wheelwrights. And all along the wide Main Street and the Broadway are pubs and lodging houses where farmers strike deals and meet their friends. If we cross the road and enter the Market Hall we see on our right a tiny jail (lockup) where farm lads who had overindulged in the town's many kinds of beers could be locked up to cool their heels. Over the lockup door is a warning carved in stone that reads 'commit no nuisance'. Committing a nuisance covered just about anything from public indecency to keeping a bawdy house, or even a large dog with a habit of biting. You can still see the sign today.

Such was the hustle and bustle of eighteenth-century Amersham on a market day. Set astride the crossroads, where the road from London to Aylesbury and Birmingham met the Hatfield to Reading turnpike, the town had been serving the needs of farmers, tradesmen and travellers for hundreds of years. Yet change was in the wind for this was the dawn of the Industrial Revolution which would propel Amersham from its rural ways to become today's shining example of a modern town, home to a leading UK life sciences company. And yet for the next 150 years the largest industry in the town was brewing. For a long time Amersham's many coaching inns, pubs and alehouses had owned their own maltings. In the early seventeenth century Amersham became famous for these malting, the largest of which supplied the local hostelries and breweries as far afield as London. In 1634 Giles Watkins built the first brewery on a site beside St Mary's Church, on the north side of the river. He died shortly afterwards and after several changes of ownership in 1775 the brewery was acquired by William Weller, a maltster from High Wycombe. Weller's Brewery became a major competitor in the Buckinghamshire and Hertfordshire beer market over the next 149 years, eventually owning 133 tied houses.

Other early industries for which Amersham was noted included lacemaking, straw plaiting and furniture-making. The town was celebrated for a particular type of black lace much in demand for veils in the seventeenth century. Lacemaking was a cottage industry. The finely stitched lace was sold to haberdashers and fashion houses in London and Paris, where it was highly prized. Straw plaiting was often a side line for the lacemakers. It was plaited into 20-yard lengths for making straw hats and most of it was sold in Luton, which, then as now, was a centre for hat making. Furniture-making never reached the scale achieved in High Wycombe, nevertheless, there were bodgers' sheds in the beech woods surrounding Amersham where the bodgers turned chair legs on treadle-driven lathes. There were also furniture factories on the outskirts of Amersham, where chairs were manufactured for sale in Amersham and in London.

At about this time the roads in this part of Buckinghamshire were 'turnpiked' – stretches of highway were leased out to individuals who could charge passing traffic, in return for which they were obliged to maintain the road. The quality of the road surfaces improved dramatically, goods were moved more easily and reliably, and Amersham's trade grew accordingly. In those

Loading bales of wool on the High Street.

An anti-free trade meeting in Amersham High Street.

A chair maker's workshop, early twentieth century.

An Amersham gamekeeper with his dog (late nineteenth century).

A chair-making factory on the outskirts of Amersham.

Removing horse manure on the High Street.

The Amersham blacksmith, *c.* 1900.

Amersham wheelwrights building a cart, late nineteenth century.

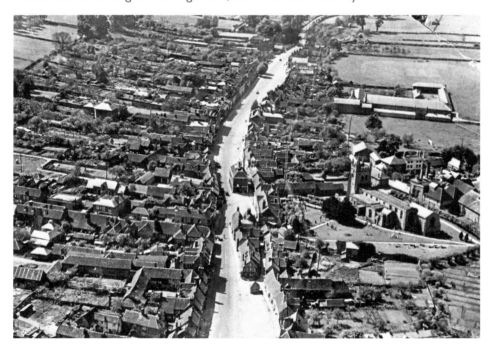

Amersham from the air in the 1920s – note the buildings in the Broadway.

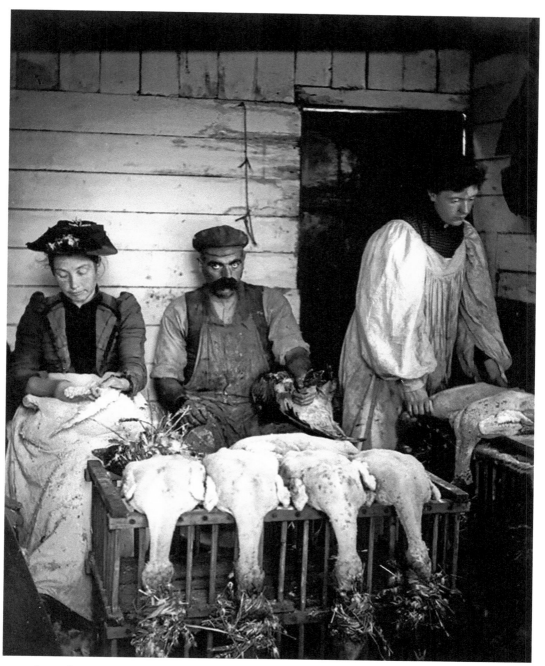

Amersham butcher plucking poultry, late nineteenth century.

The Amersham cobbler at work with his family.

Traditional farming methods lasted until the 1950s.

Traditional Amersham lacemakers.

days it would have taken the lace dealers and chair-makers about half a day to make the journey from Amersham to London.

Right up until the late nineteenth century work in Amersham had remained essentially unchanged for hundreds of years. Most of the work would have been farm labour with little change from generation to generation, governed by the seasons and starting in childhood, with long hours and little protection from unemployment. Moreover, in 1841 male life expectancy was just forty years. Those in trade, such as the merchants, shopkeepers, chair-makers, maltsters, publicans, hotel keepers and carters could aspire to some improvements in their fortunes from one generation to the next. Only landowners and professionals such as lawyers, doctors and teachers could look to a life of relative comfort and the prospect of a peaceful retirement.

Then, in 1892, everything changed when the railway arrived at what was to become Amersham-on-the-Hill. However, long before the railway transformed working life in Amersham, other enterprises sprang up in the Bury Farm area between the Chequers public house and the Broadway.

A 'bodger' turns chair legs using a treadle lathe.

Straw plaiting supplemented the income of lacemakers.

Master chair maker George Bolam finishes a commemorative bishop's chair for Preston Church near Faversham.

Weller's Brewery from the Misbourne bridge, c. 1900.

BREWING FOR BUCKINGHAMSHIRE

Since pre-Norman times Amersham has been a market town and the main commodity traded was grain, mainly wheat and barley. While much of the grain would have found its way into London, Amersham had its own grain mills. The oldest of these was Town Mill, built over the River Misbourne at the north-western end of the town. It is now a highly desirable residence. Bury Mill was located on land between Ambers and Tesco's car park. This mill functioned until the 1890s, when the building of Station Road disrupted the mill stream and the mill was closed. A third mill was built in the 1760s on land where the Amersham Recycling Centre is now located on London Road. All three mills were driven by waterwheels and at their peak produced over fifty sacks of flour per week. Looking at the River Misbourne today one might wonder how such a modest stream could have powered several watermills; however, up until the twentieth century the Misbourne was a much more vigorous river until water extraction greatly curtailed the flow, so much so that these days Thames water is piped from Medmenham to the Deep Mill reservoir on the road to Missenden to supplement the domestic water supply for Amersham.

The availability of top quality barley led to the establishment of many maltings. In these long low buildings barley was soaked in water and allowed to slowly germinate so that the starch in the grain became maltose – a key ingredient in the brewing of beer. Most of Amersham's larger pubs brewed their own beer, although since the fifteenth century a small brewery had stood beside the Misbourne where the Memorial Gardens are now located.

For many years the brewers at the Amersham brewery seemed to take a leisurely and sometimes unlawful approach to business; one Richard Tipping was prosecuted in 1728 for supplying beer to an unlicensed beer seller. However, in 1775 William Weller arrived in Amersham and purchased the brewery along with The Saracens Head in Whielden Street and the Old Griffin public house at Mop End on the High Wycombe road. For the next 150 years the Weller family grew the business to include tied houses as far away as Quainton and Harefield and become the engine of the local economy.

Throughout the nineteenth century this family business grew dramatically with the construction of new maltings on the meadow on the other side of Church Street, new stables over the road from the brewery itself, which, with the addition of a cooperage, bottling plant, warehouse and offices, became the imposing building that is now Badminton Court.

A celebrated advertising man once said 'The best way to improve the sales of a product is to improve the product'. The Wellers excelled with this strategy, brewing a variety of beers of which one, Wellers Entire, outsold all the others. It was a dark beer brewed with a rich malt and a touch of brown sugar. Its popularity drove the acquisition by the Church Street Brewery of 133 tied houses.

The management of the brewery was generous, far-sighted but paternalistic. Employees enjoyed numerous outings to the Great Exhibition and to the seaside. The work in the brewery was largely physical with few labour-saving machines; however, brewery employees were allowed to drink as much as they liked while at work. What is more, every employee was permitted to take home a gallon of beer a day. But there was to be no slacking if these dizzying perks were to be earned. One retired brewery worker recalled how in an age before wristwatches the workers took to popping out of the brewery to check the time on the clock on the north side of the tower on top of the Market Hall. The Wellers complained to the Drakes and the clock face was duly covered over. At some point it must have been uncovered because the north face of the clock is now clear for all to see.

The Weller family were also great benefactors to Amersham, providing the town with a fire brigade and land for the Amersham lawn tennis and hockey clubs.

In the 1920s, faced with increasing competition from breweries located near railway hubs and with refrigeration allowing beer to be transported over greater distances, the industry began to consolidate. In 1929 George Weller, then in his eighties and unable to find a successor in the family, sold the brewery and its 133 tied houses to Benskins Brewery in Watford. Some townspeople believed that Benskins would keep the brewery open, while others thought it would only continue to operate the bottling plant. In the event Benskins only wanted Wellers for the tied houses and within a year or two the last ever brew was bottled, the great dray horses were put out to pasture or sold, the malting kilns were doused and the Church Street brewery was closed.

The pool at the town mill.

Wellers' draymen deliver beer to an Amersham pub.

Despite generous offers (for the time) of £1 for every year worked at the brewery and a plan to sell the employees their cottages, the closure caused great bitterness and some hardship in Amersham. But by now the focus of industrial growth in the town had shifted up the hill to the new town, where the railway was bringing a whole new way of life and work.

In the decade before the Second World War the brewery was home to a badminton club and during the war troops were billeted in the building. The Maltings were requisitioned for the manufacture of parachutes and barrage balloons. Immediately after the war, when Goya Cosmetics relocated from Buckingham to the old brewery premises in Amersham, the building was renamed Badminton Court.

The old meets the new outside Weller's Brewery.

Weller's Brewery yard, *c.* 1900.

Above: The earliest known photograph of the Weller's Brewery workforce, probably taken in the mid-nineteenth century.

Right: Weller's Brewery manager with company trophies.

Amersham's first fire engine, which served the town for sixty years.

The Amersham Fire Brigade with their new engine in 1928.

Right: Amersham firefighter (early twentieth century).

Below: Amersham Market Hall photographed in the 1920s.

TOWN HALL AMERSHAM

THE BURY END OF TOWN

AMERSHAM'S 'EAST END'

It is a characteristic of many English towns and cities that the wealthy made their homes on the western side of town while the poor and industries that emitted dust, fumes and unwholesome smells – such as milling, skinning and tanning – were consigned to the eastern, downwind side. And so it was at Amersham, where some of the earliest industrial activities were located at the Bury End of town beyond the Broadway, where the prevailing wind carried pollution along the Misbourne Valley.

For centuries there had been watermills on the banks of the Misbourne and traces of the mill race that drove the wheel at one of these can be seen on the riverbank behind Tesco's car park.

For all their pastoral charm, many English country towns contained pockets of grinding poverty, particularly among agricultural labouring communities. In the late eighteenth century a Lancashire Baptist minister arrived in Amersham, bringing a knowledge of the cotton industry with him. Richard Morris determined to do something to alleviate this distress. He formed a partnership with a local man, Thomas Hailey, and together they started a factory in a converted barn at Bury End with the aim of providing employment. It grew to become the largest cotton mill in south-east England with facilities for spinning, weaving and bleaching the cotton. At the turn of the century the company employed around 100 people – a large enterprise for the time. However, Napoleon's Continental System, a continent-wide embargo on British goods imposed in retaliation for Britain's blockade of continental ports, severely damaged British trade. Morris and Hailey's cotton mill business declined and was forced to close in 1807.

The loss of this enterprise caused further hardship in the town and in an attempt to maintain employment the mill was bought by a consortium that included John and William Weller of the brewing family. But it was to no avail and the mill closed for good in 1809. Subsequently the factory and the site was purchased by the Drakes, the hereditary Lords of the Manor and owners of Shardeloes, the family seat high on the hill to the west of the town.

The cotton mill limped on with various unsuccessful attempts to keep it going until it was finally abandoned in the 1840s. History doesn't record what use was made of this early industrial site following the demise of the cotton mill – it probably reverted to farm use. However, Amersham's position at a crossroads made the town a meeting place and as transport and

Pile driving and construction of the Amersham gasometer in 1893.

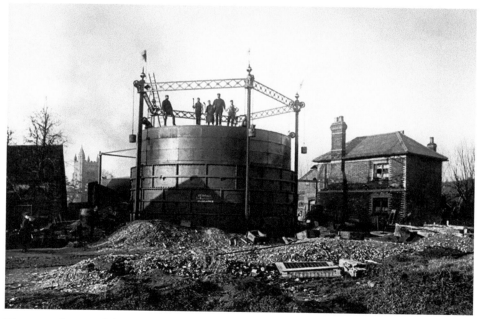

The completion of the gasometer in 1893.

Amersham gasworks in the 1920s.

roads improved the town became a transport hub for this part of Buckinghamshire. In the twentieth century, with the introduction of motor transport, the area where the Tesco petrol station now stands became an important bus station for London Country Buses with links to all the principal towns and villages in the area, eventually becoming a terminus for London Transport's Green Line suburban service. Further east on the London Road an enterprise which was to become a mainspring of the Amersham economy opened a factory where the cotton mill once stood. This factory was to drive the local economy for seventy-five years.

PIE MAKERS TO THE NATION

The story of Brazil's is an inspiring tale of family ambition, determination and ingenuity, of battling with the wartime loss of markets and the Great Depression and of opportunity seized, expansion and great commercial success. Above all it is a story of a classic family business.

The founders of Brazil's were George (the Guv'nor) and his wife Annie. George had been apprenticed in the butcher's trade in Berwick Street in London and in the 1890s they opened a butcher's shop at No. 52 the High Street, Amersham (now No. 95). They sold what was called 'Colonial Meat' because it came from Canada and the USA. This was controversial at the time because the press was bitterly opposed to importing food. George bought the meat at Smithfield Market and carried it back to Amersham in wicker baskets on the train. By the outbreak of the First World War George and Annie had ten children and the demands of looking after this large family outstripped the income from the business, despite having expanded with additional shops in Chesham and Windsor. A crisis faced the business when war came because all imports of meat products were restricted. One day Annie suggested to the Guv'nor and the boys that they should make sausages and pies. This they started to do in a makeshift factory in the stable at No. 52 High Street. They had no oven and so the pies were cooked at the nearby bakery. They pooled what money they had and bought a Model T delivery van. This proved to be the making of the Brazil's. They quickly outgrew the factory in the stable and with a nudge from the public health authorities they purchased land at Wilkins Meadow at the Bury Farm end of town, where Tesco now stands. Here they built, largely with their own hands, a factory equipped for slaughter, processing and packing an ever-increasing range of meat products, including pies, sausages, black pudding, bacon and much more.

Three of their sons, George junior, John and Ronald, expanded the business, adding buildings and new facilities, opening a branch in Winchester and acquiring a meat processing business in Witney. By now the Brazils' entrepreneurial spirit was shared by their brothers and sisters. Sidney built a garage business in Great Missenden. Robin became a property developer and built much of Stanley Hill, Dorothy opened a corsetry shop next door to the original butcher's shop on Amersham High Street. Under George's paternal leadership Brazil's became a model for modern employment practice with a cricket team, a football team and frequent outings and parties for the staff.

Clearly the Brazil clan liked a good party and their family history is full of stories of practical jokes, including cutting an unsuspecting family member's braces so his trousers fell down, squirting a prospective business partner with a hosepipe and smuggling a sedated piglet into a Beautiful Baby contest!

The north side of Amersham High Street showing the original Brazil's butcher's shop on the right.

The pie makers at work.

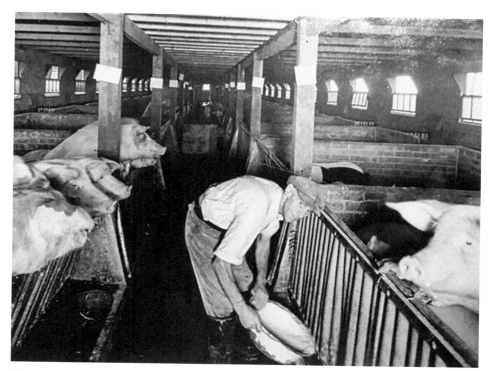

The piggery at the Brazil's factory.

The Brazil's cricket team, c. 1960.

Miss Doris Jones singing at a Brazil's Christmas party in 1938.

A combined Christmas party with staff from Amersham, Witney and Windsor in 1938.

Brazil's staff gather to hear the declaration of war with Germany, 3 September 1939.

Above: Brazil's staff dancing in the garden during the Second World War.

Left: George Brazil.

Right: John Brazil.

Below: Brazil's became a leading meat products brand and a household name after the Second World War.

The Brazil's Bowyers management team.

When the Second World War broke out in 1939 Brazil's was thriving, with a fleet of ten delivery vans and a 6-ton lorry that brought carcasses up from Smithfield Market. Now once again war and food rationing threatened the business, but with the help of John Brazil's astute salesmanship the company secured contracts with the NAAFI and the Royal Navy, quickly becoming the largest suppliers of processed meat products to the Armed Services.

The employees at Brazil's enthusiastically supported the Home Guard to such an extent that the Amersham detachment contained a unit called Brazil's Division. It is said that generous supplies of Brazil's pies to an American army unit stationed nearby paved the way to the Amersham Home Guard being the only Home Guard unit to possess a tank. A slightly more plausible version of the story tells of the Home Guard 'borrowing' a Bren Gun Carrier from a regular unit stationed in the woods opposite Shardeloes.

In 1942 the family matriarch, Annie, died and the Guv'nor passed away the following year. The loss of the founders of the business was a devastating blow to the three 'Brazil Boys'. In 1950 Ronald died. By that time Brazil's had become a national consumer brand and in some

Brazil's were famed for their staff parties.

ways the family had achieved their ambitions. However, the company needed capital to invest in the dawning consumer age of supermarkets and in 1958 Brazil's was floated on the stock exchange. Sadly, George, the eldest of the three brothers, died just as the flotation was about to take place. The company was floated but thereafter it became the repeated target for takeovers, which eventually prevailed in the late 1960s when Bowyers bought the business and the Brazil's brand.

The plant on the corner of Station Hill and the London Road continued to make pies and sausages until 1986, when production was moved elsewhere. The demolition men moved in and in 1988 the site was levelled to make way for one of the country's first Tesco superstores. Over the years Brazil's had employed many hundreds of Amersham people, some of whom had started at the butcher's shop in 1922 and served the firm until the end. If Weller's Brewery was the economic heart of Amersham in the nineteenth century, Brazil's carried it into the first half of the twentieth.

THE WORKHOUSE, WELFARE AND HEALTHCARE

A constant theme in the growth of Amersham is the encroachment of housing, industry, roads and railways on agricultural land. And from the mid-nineteenth century onwards mechanisation reduced the numbers of people working in many different trades, in industry and particularly in agriculture. So what happened to those for whom there was no work, or those widowed with children, or those who were too ill to work?

Since Elizabethan times responsibility had been placed on parishes to provide support for the poor. Benefactors such as William Drake, who inherited Shardeloes in the early seventeenth century, built almshouses; small rows of terraced houses such as can be seen on Amersham High Street and Wielden Street. Here widows, the infirm and the desperately poor could apply to be housed and fed 'on the parish'. For the most part it seems to have been an ungenerous but benign system.

However, by the end of the eighteenth century the system was collapsing with dilapidated buildings, corrupt wardens and ever-increasing demand. The years at the end of the eighteenth century were particularly hard on the poor. Several bad harvests had forced up the price of grain and bread so that they were no longer affordable for unskilled workers, farm labourers and the poor. There is evidence that soup kitchens were set up in Amersham at this time, catering for as much as 20 per cent of the population.

In the early 1800s the Revd Richard Morris set up a cotton spinning mill to provide employment but it was unable to compete and closed after just a few years.

Hitherto there had been work houses in most parishes, but with the passing of the Poor Laws the industrious Victorians set out to reform the system. However, in doing so, they brought their high-minded morality to bear on those unfortunate enough to need its services. Individual parish provision was abolished and brought together in 'unions of parishes' that would contribute to single, larger institutions. Amersham became the site of a Union that drew on funds and occupants from as far afield as Beaconsfield, Chalfont St Giles, Chesham and The Lee.

The Amersham Union, known as the 'workhouse' or 'the institution', was designed by George Gilbert Scott. It is an imposing flint faced building in the Tudor style. Ironically, today it has been converted into desirable private apartments. In its heyday it offered segregated dormitories for men, women, children and vagrants. None were excluded from work if they were sufficiently able bodied: the 8th rule of the Amersham Union Workhouse read, 'Harsh difficult work to be performed by all fit inmates'. They were encouraged in this by being turned out of the workhouse from early morning until evening. Residents unfit for work might be put to 'picking oakum'. This was a tedious and unpleasant task. Used rope was picked apart and reduced to its fibres, which were used for sealing joints in ships' timbers and in plumbing.

The unpopularity of the workhouse regime can be glimpsed in newspaper accounts of a disturbance that took place in 1835. The Union system called for the separation of men and women to different locations. That meant that impoverished families could be broken up. Public disorder flared up when men from the Chesham workhouse were being taken by cart to Amersham. Up to 100 Chesham residents protested, chasing the cart, stoning the driver and earning the ringleaders a month in jail.

The workhouse system persisted well into the twentieth century, by which time the Amersham Union had earned a reputation for relative comfort among the country's wayfarers. It was reported that 10,977 tramps stayed overnight in the Amersham Union vagrants' ward in the course of 1925.

The Gilbert Scott-designed Amersham Union in the early twentieth century.

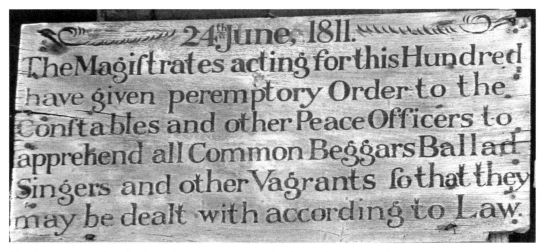

24th June, 1811. The Magistrates acting for this Hundred have given peremptory Order to the Constables and other Peace Officers to apprehend all Common Beggars Ballad Singers and other Vagrants so that they may be dealt with according to Law.

Harsh treatment for the homeless was common in the early nineteenth century.

Nurses parade on the High Street during the First World War.

The Union infirmary that eventually grew into Amersham Hospital.

In 1930 Buckinghamshire County Council took over the running of the workhouse from the Union Board of Guardians and divided it into two separate institutions; the Public Assistance Institution and the infirmary, which later became St Mary's Hospital. In 1938, as war clouds gathered, the infirmary was requisitioned and turned into an Emergency Services Hospital for military and civilian patients. A maternity department for London evacuees was set up at Shardeloes. With the introduction of the National Health Service in 1948 all the buildings were turned into hospital units and the whole site was renamed Amersham Hospital. For many years it was a general hospital offering Accident and Emergency, Maternity and General Surgery services. However, by the mid-1990s, as a result of several NHS reorganisations, Amersham became a specialised hospital with facilities for the care of the elderly, and for the treatment of skin diseases and psychiatric care.

The era of the workhouse was a grim time for the poor in the history of Amersham. And yet the pitifully inadequate infirmary provided for the inmates eventually grew into a modern hospital. Before the creation of Amersham Hospital there had been no such healthcare provision for the people of the town. Anyone suffering from serious illness or injury had to travel to High Wycombe or to Aylesbury.

THE OLD BREWERY AND MALTINGS

VITAL WAR WORK

In the Second World War many soldiers, sailors and airmen owed their lives to equipment made in the buildings of the maltings in Old Amersham. These spacious premises were converted into workshops for the manufacture of barrage balloons, inflatable dinghies, life vests – the famous Mae Wests worn by aircrew – and parachutes.

The barrage balloons were designed for convoy use to be flown from ships to deter low level attack from the air. Nearly 7,000 of these convoy balloons were made in Amersham, and over 160 men and women were employed in this vital work.

Various other unusual activities took place in Amersham during the war. Two houses in Pollards Wood were requisitioned for the training of Polish agents. They became Special Training School XX for the SOE (Special Operations Executive). Several courageous missions into occupied Poland were mounted from this location.

The managers of the barrage balloon factory in The Maltings.

Over 160 men and women worked at the balloon factory in the Second World War.

The material storeroom at The Maltings.

Above, below and opposite page: The workshops at The Maltings where convoy balloons, dinghies and life vests were manufactured.

Handling orders for equipment – note the loudspeaker.

The stores of adhesives and cordage.

A Home Guards signals unit.

Brazil's Home Guard unit parades at Affricks Farm commanded by George Brazil on the right.

The Amersham Home Guard.

Next-door neighbours to the Polish special agents were the animals and performers of Bertram Mills Circus, resident in Pollards Wood for the duration of the war. Periodically the circus travelled by train from Little Chalfont to perform elsewhere in the country. Wartime residents of Little Chalfont recall the elephants walking along the main street, each holding the tail of the animal ahead, the procession eagerly watched by hopeful allotment keepers with buckets and shovels hoping for a hefty deposit of manure to be left on the road.

The Amersham Home Guard was a formidable force by the end of the war and performed important defensive duties for the large contingents of D-Day invasion forces training in camps in Rectory Woods and elsewhere in the Amersham area. The war was also the catalyst that transformed the Amersham Union Infirmary into an Emergency Military Hospital, which eventually became Amersham General Hospital.

COSMETICS IN THE SWINGING SIXTIES

The next successful enterprise to lend a shoulder to the wheel of the Amersham economy was a far cry from brewing and meat processing.

In 1936 a young entrepreneur named Douglas Collins decided to try his hand in the perfume business. Living and working in Kentish Town he created fifteen experimental perfumes and explored the secrets of the perfume trade. His breakthrough came in 1938 when *Women's Journal* magazine ran a circulation-boosting promotion using tiny sample vials of perfume as a giveaway with every copy of the magazine – supplied by Douglas Collins. During the Second World War Collins served in the Royal Navy but his business continued to thrive in his absence. At the outbreak of war the company letterhead showed a prestigious Piccadilly address but the threat of bombing persuaded the management to move the business to Buckingham. By the end of the war turnover had reached an impressive £250,000 a year. When Paris fell the firm ran an advertisement that read, 'Goodbye Paris But Goya is a luxury that is still in perfect taste.'

Douglas Collins, the founder of Goya Cosmetics.

Returning from naval service Collins realised the business needed larger premises if it was to meet the growing demand in the UK and overseas. So in 1946 Goya Cosmetics (as they were now called) moved into the old Weller's Brewery buildings (by now refurbished as offices and workshops and renamed Badminton Court). By 1951 turnover had reached over £600,000.

The Goya business had enjoyed great success during the war. Understandably women and men sought what little romance they could find in a time of separations and austerity. A little lipstick and a dab of perfume worked wonders for wartime morale. In the 1950s and '60s the world discovered youth markets and young women, empowered by their war work experiences and now with a disposable income, eagerly sought Goya's moderately priced quality products. The company reached its zenith in the 1970s with product offers that matched the mood of flower-power Britain. But ultimately Goya was unable to challenge the great French and American perfume houses or to meet the competition from new even more youthful brands such as Boots No7, Rimmel and Mabelline.

However, Douglas Collins was a determined and energetic perfumier. At his Badminton Court HQ he created a 'fragrance organ'. This was a workstation with an array of all the essential oils for formulating fragrances. There was very little science in it. Collins simply explored by trial and error the effects of innumerable combinations of fragrances. His close associate Ernie Joyner, a chemist, was responsible for scaling up the formulations to production quantities. This was done in a specially built compounding laboratory located in the garden behind Badminton Court. Two of their products enjoyed outstanding market success: the Black Rose range and Aqua Manda. Goya also achieved great commercial success

Badminton Court, the headquarters of Goya Cosmetics.

Special feature—Focus on Amersham

Rear view of Badminton Court from across the Misbourne.

Experimenting with different fragrance combinations.

The Goya graphic design team.

A Goya staff party, c. 1965.

The Goya sales team. Douglas Collins is seated second from the right.

The Goya girls packing cosmetics.

A Goya girls' reunion at the Crown Hotel, Amersham.

Left: The Goya netball team.

Below: Christopher Collins selecting fragrances.

Christopher Collins, who succeeded Douglas as managing director.

Classic '60s graphics on the cover of a Goya beauty guide.

with product lines such as Gardenia, English Rose, Studio and other cosmetic products marketed under the Goya name. These included lipsticks, bath salts, face powders and toilette waters. A men's range included Cedar Wood, Corvette, Sandalwood and Zendiq aftershaves, soaps and talcum powder.

In 1952 Goya opened a branch factory on Raans Road. By now Goya employed over 100 people. It was one of the first companies in the country to give employees three weeks holiday (two weeks having been normal practice up until then).

In 1960 Douglas Collins sold Goya to Reckitt & Colman for £1.5 million and eight years later bought it back from them for £800,000. Shortly after the buy-back Collins died at the age of 59 and his son, Christopher, took over as Managing Director. So began a long period of mergers and restructuring that perhaps recognised that Goya had reached its limitations as a family business but finding a comfortable niche in a large corporate structure proved elusive. Eventually the company was sold to ICI, who intended to merge Goya with a subsidiary that made Savlon medical products.

Christopher Collins is a mercurial character with wide-ranging interests. As well as being an enthusiastic sailor he also loved horses, riding in the Grand National and representing Britain in three-day equestrian events. His business interests spread beyond Goya with directorships of Hanson Group and Suttons Seeds. In 1982, in a message to employees, Goya's Chief Executive said that it had been a difficult year. A brief period of sharp decline followed and the number of employees fell from 179 to 151. By now Goya fragrances accounted for less than a third of company sales. Profitability evaporated. In 1984 the company was sold to Beauty International and the Goya factories and offices at Badminton Court and Raans Road were closed for the last time.

And yet, as is so often the case, the brand lives on long after the company has vanished. Today, resurrected Aqua Manda and Black Rose products can still be found. For many the name Goya still resonates with the music, fashion and freedom of the 1960s and '70s, and a generation of Amersham employees who worked at Goya look back fondly at the heady days of the town's international success in the cosmetics business.

AMERSHAM-ON-THE-HILL

A NEW WAY OF LIFE AND WORK

In Thomas Hardy's *Jude the Obscure*, Jude suggests to Sue Bridehead that they go and sit in the Cathedral together: 'I think I'd rather sit in the railway station,' she replies. 'That's the centre of the town life now.'

For hundreds of years market town life continued undisturbed in the Old Town of Amersham, and then the railway arrived, utterly transforming both the way of life and the way of working in the town. It was a giant leap into the twentieth century. The Metropolitan Railway first ran from Baker Street to Farringdon in the City in the 1860s. In 1887 the line extended north-west to reach Rickmansworth and Chalfont Road, now called Chalfont & Latimer. From there the route of the line was much disputed. One faction wanted the line to run to Tring via Chesham and two years later it did reach Chesham. Meanwhile the Tyrwhitt-Drakes of Shardeloes objected to the line running along the Misbourne Valley to Aylesbury via Amersham (the route selected for the present day HS2). They disliked the idea of looking out from their manor house high over Old Amersham at the huffing and puffing of steam trains in the valley below.

Eventually the decision was made to construct a line from Chalfont Road to Aylesbury with a station in what must have seemed like the middle of nowhere on Amersham Common, a mile away from Old Amersham. And so it was that on the 1 September 1892 Amersham was finally connected by rail with the metropolis.

Yet that decision is probably what saved Old Amersham from being swamped by suburban housing and industrial development. And at the same time it provided space at Amersham-on-the-Hill (as it came to be known) for that same suburban housing and industrial development to be imaginatively planned and to become the essence of John Betjeman's celebrated Metro-land.

But first the line had to be constructed. Oral testimonies on file at Amersham Museum include the recollection of a workman who quit farm labouring for 2 pence a day to work on the new line for 3½ pence a day. He remembered getting up at 5 a.m. at his home in Coleshill and walking, rain or shine, to Chorleywood for work. And if it was deemed too wet to work he didn't get paid: a stark reminder of just how hard working life was for the rural poor.

When the railway station opened the only road between Old Amersham and the New Town (as it was also sometimes called) was Rectory Hill – narrow, winding and very steep.

So Station Road was built, linking the station with the London Road at the foot of the hill. Of course few people lived in Amersham Common at that time so early efforts to boost railway traffic included the carriage of live pigs from London. They were herded down Station Road to Brazil's meat processing factory, from whence they emerged cooked and encased in pastry. Another useful and even more malodorous commodity brought up from London and eagerly sought by the farming community was an inexhaustible supply of horse manure from the city streets. In 1898 *The Times* estimated that central London streets would be 9 feet deep in horse manure by 1950. *Scientific American* drily noted, 'The improvement in city conditions by the general adoption of the motorcar can hardly be overestimated.'

In 1893 Weller's Brewery built The Station Hotel facing the station forecourt. Two things now drove the dramatic growth of Amersham-on-the-Hill. Firstly, the Metropolitan Railway went into the property development business partly using surplus land acquired for the building of the railway line and partly buying up land within walking distance of the station. They built houses and offered them for sale with mortgages included. Secondly, thousands of office workers and professionals began to move from the inner suburbs and the crowded streets of east London to Amersham, enticed by the promise of countryside, home comfort

Carpenters building Amersham Station in the 1880s.

The engine 'Caldew' and crew laying track north of Amersham in 1891.

Country life and suburban living sometimes clashed.

Country life: Boys help with
the hay-making in the 1950s.

A 1920s poster selling the
idea of living in Metro-land.

One of the first modernist country houses in Britain. It was praised by the poet John Betjeman.

and commutability. It was boom time along Sycamore Road, Hill Avenue, Woodside and Plantation Road. Before the railway came the population of Amersham was around 2,800. By 1901 it had grown to over 10,000. In 1915 the Metropilitan Railway's publicity department coined the word 'Metro-land'. It summed up all that we understand about commuting and countryside.

Opportunities for work abounded in the rapidly expanding town. Shopkeepers moved up the hill from Old Amersham to serve the new residents and shop assistants easily found work in the seventy shops that opened there by 1924. Six years later that number had more than doubled to 170.

The building trade grew too, with over 2,500 houses built in the decade after the First World War. At the height of the boom local builder Alfred Woodley employed over 100 people, and local architects began to develop the four designs of classic Metro-land three-bedroom detached and semi-detached houses with hipped roofs, faux half-timbered gables and – to the delight of their new owners – gardens. Between 1929 and 1931 Amyas Connell, an architect from New Zealand, designed a new house for the distinguished archaeologist Professor Bernard Ashmole. Connell was greatly influenced by the work of Le Corbusier and the result was one of the earliest 'modernist international style' country houses in England. Internationally acclaimed and adored by John Betjeman, High & Over (as the house is called) stands in a spectacular position on the slopes above Station Road overlooking the Misbourne Valley and the Old Town.

Yet the most significant change for the way Amersham people now lived and worked was that many didn't work in Amersham at all. They disappeared during the day to work in banking, insurance and shipping in the City of London (or, in the case of Professor Ashmole, to the British Museum). Amersham had become a dormitory town.

GOING TO WORK ON THE TRAIN

Today commuting by train is seen as a necessary evil; it's that 'dead time' between the clamour for the bathroom, a frantic breakfast and packing the children off to school and logging on at a workstation far away while surreptitiously checking to see who is already in the office and who will be late. It's a time of reduced personal space, of resentment towards luggage and conversation, for crosswords, Sudoku and revisiting the best of *Breaking Bad* on a tablet. The return journey is not much better: sitting slack-jawed in shallow sleep until woken by force of habit at your destination. But it wasn't like this in the early days.

It was new and exciting to think that great distances that would have taken most of the day to travel by horse-drawn coach could now be crossed in time for a full day's work and still return home in time for an evening with the family. And it could be done every working day in the year for an annual cost of just £48.

As the Metropolitan line reached Amersham so the Great Central Railway made its way south from Sheffield, Nottingham and Leicester via Rugby, Quainton Road, Aylesbury and Amersham to Marylebone, sharing the southern end of the line with the Metropolitan line into Baker Street.

Smart steam locomotives in green livery hauled chocolate and cream-coloured carriages, some of which were Pullman dining cars, with morning and evening services stopping at Amersham for well-to-do City bankers and stockbrokers. In the 1950s famous trains such as The Master Cutler and The South Yorkshireman from Sheffield flew through Amersham en route to London.

In the 1930s the Metropolitan line was electrified to Rickmansworth and trains travelling beyond there switched to a steam locomotive for the onward journey north and vice versa. But the writing was on the wall for the Great Central Railway because it was considered to be a duplication of other northern routes. It was eventually incorporated into the London North Eastern Railway (LNER) and then merged with the Metropolitan Railway as traffic declined. Eventually the line north of Aylesbury was closed by Dr Beeching. And so the present-day pattern of train services came into being with London Underground operating from Baker Street over lines to Amersham, which were finally electrified in 1960, and Chiltern Railways operating from Marylebone to Aylesbury via Amersham.

Of course not all commuters travelled in first-class Pullman cars with a steward in a starched white jacket in attendance. The bulk of Amersham's new residents who rode the

A driver and fireman pose with their steam locomotive at Amersham Station.

Express trains from London to Sheffield ran through Amersham in the 1920s.

The first telephone exchange in Amersham was installed in 1902; there were thirteen subscribers.

The Henry Appleby and track-laying crew near Amersham in the 1880s.

trains to work in London were the clerks, managers, traders, buyers, tellers, secretaries, shippers, shopkeepers and civil servants that made the City tick.

Spending the working day in London was to enter a different and somewhat isolated world. In the days before mobile phones and personal computers the office telephone was strictly a business tool. Private phone calls would not normally be permitted. So the commuters' world of work would be completely cut off from home town and family life. At lunchtime the hungry commuter could eat at places like the ABC Restaurants. With the capacity to seat over 1,000 diners, the ABC would serve a simple canteen-style meal. To pay for it firms provided their staff with Luncheon Vouchers. These were a tax-free perk. The vouchers became a kind of currency and could be used to purchase many things that had little to do with lunch (as was revealed in the scandalous prosecution of Mrs Cynthia Payne, whose South London bordello accepted Luncheon Vouchers for sexual services). The maximum value of Luncheon Vouchers given to each employee was three shillings per day.

If trains were delayed or a sudden strike brought services to a halt the only means of communicating was by public telephone. In the 1950s, calling Amersham would have involved putting the money for the call into a slot and pressing a button marked 'A', lifting the receiver and dialling '0' to speak to an operator. If the call could not be connected the caller could press a similar button marked 'B' to get their money back. It was not unusual for someone waiting to make a call to bang on the telephone box window to hurry the current caller along. Before the Second World War telephones in private homes were a rarity, although they would have appeared in many private homes in Amersham in the 1950s. The Bakelite instrument would have held pride of place in the hall.

If John Betjeman was the supreme eulogiser of Metro-land, perhaps the greatest chronicler of working life for City commuters was Frank Dickens, whose strip cartoon character Bristow appeared in the *Evening Standard* for over fifty years. The downtrodden but rebellious buying clerk at the Chester Perry Organisation perfectly captured the world of commuting and office work with its thwarted ambitions and petty rivalries under the ferocious boss, Head Buyer Fudge. But for Bristow all was redeemed by the periodic visits of Miss Pretty from Kleenaphone. No doubt in real life many a Miss Pretty would have met her buying clerk at work in the City, married and settled down to family life in a Woodley Home in Amersham-on-the-Hill.

In these ways the world of work for the people of Amersham, and the town itself, changed beyond recognition from that of the agricultural workers. But if steam engines wrought such change and created new opportunities for the people of Amersham-on-the-Hill, they also challenged the working lives of farm workers in an even more direct manner. At the heart of this challenge stood Boughton's, a business born on the outskirts of Amersham-on-the-Hill.

EAST ALONG THE WHITE LION ROAD

BOUGHTON'S: STEAM IN THE VEINS

Picture a small boy in the 1880s sitting on the wall of a mill race watching the energy of the River Chess turning a waterwheel. And inside the mill marvelling at how that rotation was converted by cogs and shafts to millstones that ground the corn at Chenies Mill. The small boy was Thomas Boughton, the son of John Boughton, a tenant farmer on the Chenies Manor estate who farmed a large area of land along the Chess Valley and who owned Chenies Mill. Thomas grew up fascinated by engineering at a time when Britain's industry ruled the world, and steam was the motive power of the age. Reflecting his son's enchantment with all things steam-driven and engineered, in 1897 John Boughton purchased a steam traction engine at the Royal Counties Agricultural Show in Reading and gave it to his son. With it he bought an American-made threshing machine.

John Boughton's shrewd plan was to capitalise on his son's engineering talent and also to introduce the productivity of steam power to his farmlands. The first of over a dozen traction engines eventually owned by the newly formed T.T. Boughton was called 'Black Jack'. Restored to its former glory, Black Jack still makes appearances at Steam Fairs and County Shows.

Thomas quickly adapted the traction engine to perform numerous tasks on the farm, from threshing corn and pumping water, to drawing a plough, sawing timber and road haulage. Quick to seize an opportunity, in the 1890s Thomas persuaded the railway company to build a new siding at Chalfont Road station (now Chalfont & Latimer). The siding facilitated the arrival of thousands of tons of London horse manure, which was transferred to trailers hauled by Boughton traction engines for distribution by road to farms in the area. No doubt the draymen at Weller's Brewery would have looked on thoughtfully as Black Jack also took on the haulage of beer from pub to pub. As early twentieth-century photographs show, these leviathans could weigh up to 22 tons and played havoc with roads and bridges built for horse-drawn traffic. In these early days the seeds of many of Boughton's later successes were sown in the adaptation of vehicles for specialised applications and the handling of waste.

In the first decade of its existence T.T. Boughton was based at the family farm at Chenies, much to the disapproval of the landlord, the Duke of Bedford. His dislike of smoky, whistling steam engines and the din of metal bashing forced the Boughton's to seek new premises. These they found on Bell Lane between Amersham and Little Chalfont.

Here the emphasis of the business began to shift away from traction engines toward more general contracting work. All but one of the traction engines were sold and the company began to focus on clearing forests for building land and road rolling; both much in demand as the expansion of Amersham-on-the-Hill spread across Amersham Common. In the years before the Second World War Boughton's was also heavily engaged in clearing land for new airfields.

When war came in 1939 it brought a revival in the demand for steam power on the land and renewed opportunity for T. T. Boughton & Co. The company became a government contractor responsible for turning large areas of common and waste land into productive agricultural land. By the end of the war Boughton's had modernised their tractor fleet, which was now diesel-powered, and began to explore the possibilities of vehicle adaptation, which was to prove immensely successful in the 1960s and '70s. The first of these adaptations were winches fitted to vehicles. By the mid-1950s there were ninety variations of Boughton winch selling well at home and abroad.

The 1950s and '60s saw considerable expansion and diversification. Using the skills and experience developed during the war, Boughton's became adept at modifying vehicles and providing working attachments such as grabs, hoists and winches for the forestry industry. The product range later expanded to include cranes, oil-drilling equipment and all-wheel-drive conversions for commercial chassis. Specialist vehicle manufacture for the military market became an important activity. Perhaps inspired by the horse manure venture of the 1890s, Boughton's developed specialised vehicles for handling building waste. The first skip loader rolled out of the workshop in 1956. It was followed by a cavalcade of waste collection, compacting and fire service machines. The latter became a line of airport crash tenders designated Griffin (named after the hotel in Amersham), Pegasus, Marlin and Barracuda. Almost every airport in Britain and many airports around the world were equipped with these life-saving vehicles. Motorway construction boomed in the 1960s and '70s and Boughton's technology supported the building programme with innovations such as large load-bearing 'dollies' that supported the ends of reinforced concrete beams as they were driven from factory to bridge-building site. In 1977 the company's success in overseas markets was recognised with the prestigious Queen's Award for Export Achievement.

A stream of innovative specialised vehicles poured out of Boughton's factories, which now included three satellite plants, one of which was at Winkleigh in Devon. Vehicles included municipal waste handling trucks, fire engines, and a parade of military vehicles with hoists, dump buckets and bridging equipment. Boughton's even won a contract to convert Oskosh trucks for carrying ISO containers for the United Sates Marine Corps. By now the company employed over 500 people and was the mainspring of the Amersham economy. Its reputation for ingenious adaptation of vehicles for specialist use was second to none.

So it was a great shock to the people of Amersham to learn in 1997 that the company was in financial difficulty. The cost and complexity of delivering such an expansive range of specialised products combined with a severe credit squeeze forced the owners to sell to a venture capital company. Boughton's soldiered on under new management for a while but eventually the firm was sold again to the Skan Group, and the manufacturing plant in Amersham was relocated to Wolverhampton. The fabrication plant at Winkleigh moved to Bideford. It was a sad end to 100 years of mechanical engineering and industrious business that spanned the industrial era from steam power to computerisation. John Boughton's grandchildren, Trafford and John, were the last of the family to work in the business. In the 1980s John wrote two books about the company, *Steam in the Veins* and *Triumphs of Transport*. Lovingly maintained, Black Jack

Left: Thomas Boughton, the man with steam in his veins.

Below: 'Black Jack' at a country show in 1948.

A Boughon's traction engine driving a threshing machine, *c.* 1900.

Above: Using a steam traction engine to haul a plough.

Below: Powering a threshing machine.

Black Jack hauls dung from Chalfont Road Station in the 1890s.

A Boughton's steam lorry in the 1930s.

After the Second World War the Boughton's fleet became wholly diesel powered.

steams on as a symbol of Boughton's extraordinary contribution to the Amersham economy and the working lives of the people. The brand name Boughton's also lives on as Boughton Engineering Ltd, the Midlands-based manufacturer of the ubiquitous waste collection trucks that call on every household in the country: a fitting legacy for a company that made such a singular contribution to the relief of waste in London's nineteenth-century streets.

SHOPS AND SHOPKEEPERS

Between 1892, when the railway came to Amersham-on-the-Hill, and 1924 seventy shops opened on Sycamore Road and Hill Avenue. By the end of the 1930s there were over 170 shops in the area. The town sported a cinema – the Regent – and many shops with household names including Sainsbury's, Currys, International Stores, Jaeger and the National Provincial Bank. In recent times the toy retailer The Entertainer, which started with a small shop on Sycamore Road, has become an outstanding international success.

Gary Grant, the founder of The Entertainer, recalls how at the age of 7 he saw a 10-shilling box of chocolates in the window of a shop in Little Chalfont and promised himself he would buy it for his mother. But how? There was very little money at home, let alone pocket money, so he determined to earn it. Knocking on the door of the largest house in the neighbourhood, Gary asked the owner for work and was rewarded with odd jobs that, after a few weeks, earned the money to buy the chocolates. Gary uses this story to explain how the link between ambition, work, reward and generosity became a guiding principle, driving his ability to make money and to do good things with it.

The Entertainer is one of a long line of successful family businesses that have powered the Amersham economy, including the Wellers, the Brazils, the Boughtons, the Woodleys and the Collinses. Today the company turns over £170 million per year and employs over 2,000 people at 140 stores in the UK and twelve stores abroad. Indirectly the company employs a further 60–200 people through its independent logistics operation.

While still at school Gary did a paper round, collected empty bottles for the deposits, worked on a milk float, served in a sweet shop and at Dee's Bicycle shop on Hill Avenue. On leaving school with one O level he joined the bike shop and worked there for three years as the owner rode the boom in skateboards. When that fad declined Gary bought the surplus stock to sell privately. And that gave him enough money to start his own business.

Like many of the illustrious family businesses in Amersham's working history, the success of Gary Grant's Entertainer owes a lot to the partnership between himself and his wife Catherine. In 1981 the couple jumped at the chance to buy the Pram and Toy Bar, a toyshop on Sycamore Road, whose owner, George Marks, was retiring.

Nowadays the Grants are renowned for their business success, their charitable work and for the strong ethical beliefs that guide their business, but Gary freely admits that in the first ten years of The Entertainer he was mainly focussed on making money. In that first decade the business grew rapidly and in 1985 the shop moved to larger premises on Hill Avenue and opened a branch in Beaconsfield.

At about that time Gary became what he describes as a 'charismatic Christian'. His conversion brought about dramatic change at The Entertainer, sparking a new ethical policy, laying the foundations for a distinctive business culture and embarking on a lifelong commitment to charitable giving. The new ethical policy banned toys associated with the occult and mystical powers. Out went Halloween paraphernalia, trolls and – bravely from a business standpoint – Harry Potter merchandise. The new business culture put a premium on reputation, integrity and generosity. A Family Charter committed the company to keeping all shops closed on Sundays. The Entertainer also donates 10 per cent of its profits to charity and manages a payroll-giving scheme in which 45 per cent of employees participate. Charities the company supports include many children's hospitals and hospices, Workaid and the Scouts, whom Gary says gave him his moral compass.

An unexpected result of The Entertainer's ethical approach are the locations of the company's twelve international outlets; Cyprus, Azerbaijan and Pakistan. In these countries The Entertainer offers franchises with leading department stores. The franchisees receive a complete package, from branding and décor to products and principles. The aim is to cultivate toy retailing expertise where none has existed and equally importantly to make money and do good things with it.

Admirable principles can go a long way in business but what commercial insights have delivered such spectacular success for The Entertainer? According to Gary understanding the market is crucial and that means seeing things from a child's point of view. He illustrates this with an anecdote about a shop assistant ignoring a child at the front of the queue to serve an adult next in line behind him. Seeing this, Grant arranged for a step to be installed to bring any child waiting to pay fully into view.

The man who opened for business over thirty-five years ago with no knowledge of the industry points to four factors that have given The Entertainer a consistent competitive advantage. The first is competitive pricing and value for money. The second is the store setting; the layout, lighting and merchandising. The third is the atmosphere created by friendly, service-minded staff. And the fourth is the selection of toys on display.

Today the company's headquarters stands on the site of the old Boughton's engineering works on Bell Lane. With the worldwide toy industry growing at a rate of 6 per cent and with 20 per cent of company sales online, the future prospects for The Entertainer look good. It might surprise many who remember the little Amersham toyshop on Sycamore Road that The Entertainer is fast becoming yet another national household brand name born in Amersham, a fact eloquently expressed by the company's logo, a jack-in-the-box.

Back in the Bury End of The Old Town a retailer has ridden the post-war wave of interest in outdoor pursuits, from skiing and climbing to camping and walking. The success of Fox's, now located in front of the Tesco superstore, reflects Amersham's position as a centre for hill walking in the Chilterns. Today parties of hikers can regularly be seen leaving Amersham station and heading for the hills.

Arthur Fox started the business back in 1945, but it was more about cars than clothing in the early days. Fox's Driving School – The Chiltern School of Motoring – grew to eventually become one of the largest driving schools in the country with a fleet of fifteen cars. However, in 1956 the company had to brake sharply when the Suez Crisis brought petrol shortages and rationing, forcing the family to seek other opportunities. Mrs Ivy Fox had experience in retailing and so it was decided to open a gentleman's outfitters. Much of the early merchandise was

The Regent Cinema on Sycamore Road opened in 1928 and closed in 1962.

Above: The family business: Gary and Catherine Grant with sons Stuart (left) and Duncan (right).

The Entertainer is a £120-million business with 152 outlets managed from this HQ building on Bell Lane.

Darth Vader visits the original The Entertainer shop on Sycamore Road.

The Entertainer first moved to Hill Avenue…

…and then expanded around the corner in Sycamore Road.

At The Entertainer child steps bring customers into a shop assistant's view.

The shop window of The Entertainer when it first opened on Sycamore Road in 1981.

A Triumph Mayflower of Fox's Chiltern School of Motoring in the 1950s.

The driving school fleet in the 1950s.

The Fox family with members of the staff (Arthur Fox is third from the left).

Christmas at Fox's in the 1970s.

Chris Bonnington opens the new Fox's Outdoor Centre in front of Tesco.

military surplus clothing and camping equipment. That line of business proved very popular (a pullover cost 12 shillings and sixpence – about 60p) and Fox's began to specialise in outdoor clothing. Later the family opened a footwear shop.

In 1980 Arthur Fox died and although the driving school had recovered from the Suez debacle the family decided to close it and to bring the footwear and outdoor businesses together. In 1992 a custom-designed outdoor equipment and footwear centre was opened by Chris Bonnington, the mountaineer.

Today Fox's Outdoor is a leading brand in a highly competitive market with a growing internet business and customers from all over the country. Once again an Amersham family showed how determination and the courage to keep going and try different things eventually evolved into a leading market retailer with unrivalled knowledge in a specialist field.

AMERSHAM IN THE SECOND INDUSTRIAL REVOLUTION

GE Healthcare is by far the largest enterprise ever to have prospered in the Amersham area. Yet it all began with an HM Customs raid on a Portuguese ship in the London Docks in 1940 and a pub lunch at the White Lion on the A404.

Before the war, a long-established company called Thorium Ltd, based in Wembley, produced luminous paint for the defence establishment, but the radium to make the paint was in short supply. In the first year of the war, acting on intelligence reports, customs officers intercepted a consignment of radium concentrate aboard a Portuguese ship bound for Germany. The British government chose Thorium Ltd to process the captured material. Richard Bennet, general manager of Thorium Ltd, recruited Dr Patrick Grove to be chemist in charge of radium extraction. When bombs fell on Wembley, uncomfortably close to the Thorium laboratory, Bennet and Grove drove out of London to find new premises, close enough to London but far enough away from the bombs. They were looking for a house called Chilcote House and over lunch at the White Lion enquired as to its whereabouts. 'Next door,' they were told. They bought the house for £600. And so the seed was sown in Little Chalfont for a massive global business that would play a pioneering role in the application of particle physics in modern medicine.

To understand the nature of the work begun by Dr Grove it is not necessary to understand particle physics (although it helps!). Pioneers in this field, such as Madame Curie, had discovered radiation, X-rays and three types of atomic radiation – Alpha, Beta and Gamma rays. It had been shown that some of these rays passing through the human body revealed changes in tissue density and therefore showed the location and shape of lesions, tumours and other abnormalities. To make the radioactive substances that emitted these useful rays safe for patient consumption the substances themselves had to be exposed to radiation to alter their atomic mass so that they would quickly decay – and therefore pose no threat to the patient. These atomically altered substances are called isotopes. Today GE Healthcare make an array of isotopes designed to diagnose specific medical conditions. They also develop and manufacture scanners, of which the MRI scanner is the best known.

The relationship between isotope and scanner is this: the diagnostic process requires the patient to be administered a specific isotope, orally or by injection, and when it reaches the affected part of the body the patient is placed in a scanner which analyses the electromagnetic rays emanating from the isotope and displays the result as an image on a computer screen. This link between radiopharmaceuticals and the scanners that read their emissions was eventually to be the connection that propelled the business founded at Chilcote House into the stratosphere of global healthcare companies.

But all this lay in the future when Dr Grove moved into Chilcote House. Using the radium source seized by customs officers, Thorium Ltd expanded production, supplying luminous paint for aircraft instruments, compasses, watches and bomb sights. At the end of the war Chilcote House was purchased from Thorium Ltd by the Ministry of Supply. Thorium was appointed to manage the operation of what had become 'the national centre for the processing and distribution of radium and artificial radioactive substances for scientific, medical and industrial purposes.'

Medical applications were not the only uses for The Radiochemical Centre's isotopes. Beta and Gamma rays could be used by industry for the continuous control of thickness in sheet products such as paper and plastics, checking packaged products for desired content levels, and for eliminating static on production lines.

By the mid-1950s the company exported isotopes to over forty countries. Some of these were carried in wingtip containers installed in BOAC Bristol Britannias. Sales soon reached £1 million per year and new laboratories were built on the 7-acre Chilcote House site. The world's first commercial Cyclotron was installed. This was an electromagnetic accelerator which ensured a stable supply of isotopes for the company's medical products. The firm's meteoric growth gathered pace. By the time the first episode of *Coronation Street* was aired on ITV in 1960, exports had climbed to 60 per cent of sales, the company had over 2,000 products in its catalogue, 20,000 patients around the world were making use of isotopes made in Little Chalfont, and 450 people went to work every day at the offices and laboratories on White Lion Road. In 1967 The Radiochemical Centre received the first of fourteen Queen's Awards for Exports and Technology. Three years later The Centre became the Radiochemical Centre Limited, with Dr Grove as Managing Director. Sales topped £6 million and the number of employees went up to 1,000. In 1979 Dr Patrick Grove, founder and inspirational leader of the organisation for forty years, retired.

In the spring of 1982 the most spectacular, and for some the most controversial, change in the company's fortunes took place. The Radiochemical Centre Limited was renamed Amersham International and became the first of the Thatcher government privatisations as Amersham International Plc. It was spectacular because it was over twenty-four times oversubscribed, the value of the company increased by 34 per cent overnight, gave 99 per cent of employees a stake in the company and laid the foundations for unprecedented growth in the coming decade. It was controversial because many in politics and the press deplored the sale of state assets and complained that the offer had been priced too low. It was an argument that was to resurface twelve years later when the company merged with GE Healthcare.

Various business developments now appeared in the annual reports; laboratories were opened in Cardiff and in Gloucester, the United States Biochemical Corporation was acquired and the company merged with Nycomed of Norway and then with Pharmacia Biotech of Sweden, creating the world's largest diagnostic imaging business (bringing X-ray technology under the Amersham umbrella).

To handle the rapidly expanding organisation Amersham International built a new headquarters at Amersham Place in Little Chalfont, noted by near neighbours for the eye-catching blue machinery space on the roof.

Three years after the privatisation the assets of the company had risen to £100 million, the number of staff members had tripled and the company was pouring 10 per cent of sales into research and development. Amersham had never seen anything like it.

Amersham International now faced a strategic dilemma; either find partners with whom the company could achieve market leadership in diagnostics and life sciences, or vertically integrate the business into engineering and digitalisation.

Under the leadership of the then CEO, Sir William Martin Castell, the company chose the latter path. Consequently, in 2004, Amersham International Plc was acquired by General Electric of the United States for £5.7 billion. The acquisition brought together GE's medical imaging equipment and Amersham's medical diagnostic and life sciences businesses. The new global company was called GE Healthcare. It was the first ever GE business with headquarters outside the United States. It is the key event that helped to make the dream of a $15 billion (£11.6 billion) medical technology business a reality. It was also the first step in the realisation of a vision of totally personalised patient treatment based on integrated genetics, diagnostics, engineering and information technology.

This vision has already turned GE Healthcare into an $18 billion (£14 billion) worldwide business with over 50,000 employees. The Chilcote House location on White Lion Road, now renamed The Grove Centre, remains one of GE Healthcare's principal sites, home to manufacturing, distribution and the research and development of new diagnostic imaging agents.

The roll call of scientific progress at Amersham International and GE Healthcare is phenomenal. The company provides medical imaging and information technologies, medical diagnostics, patient monitoring systems, drug discovery, and biopharmaceutical manufacturing technologies.

Vios Works is a device that extends magnetic resonance assessment to provide cardiovascular images in a fraction of the time taken by conventional scans.

Silent Scan, developed in 2012, reduced the noise made by MRI scanners from heavy metal levels to a whisper – hitherto a common source of patient complaint. The discomforts of mammograms can now be managed with Senographe Pristina, a mammography system that allows women to control breast compression themselves. Vscan is a portable mini ultrasound unit that doctors and midwives can carry with them. This has made ultrasound scans more readily available in developing countries, bringing better pregnancy care to millions of mothers-to-be.

As to the future, GE Healthcare is investing $500 million (£390 million) in digital technology. The extraordinary success of Amersham International and GE Healthcare has enabled the company to support the communities in which it operates not just locally but nationally and internationally too. Among many other charitable activities, GE Healthcare has supported the Pride of Bucks Awards for the community's unsung heroes and is active

Dr Patrick Grove, the visionary who saw the possibilities for isotopes in medicine.

Chilcote House, where it all started.

in supporting Help for Heroes – the fundraising campaign for wounded ex-servicemen and women.

GE also invests heavily in education and skills. As the third largest industrial company in the UK it is focused on encouraging more young people to study STEM subjects (Science, Technology, Engineering and Maths), particularly concentrating on opportunities for girls.

It is a long journey from the manufacture of luminous dials to a front line role in the world's battle with diseases, such as cancer, diabetes, heart disease and dementia. Amersham can be proud of hosting such an innovative and successful business and to have provided the working base for visionaries like Dr Patrick Grove, who saw the potential in radioactive imaging products.

It has also been a long journey from working life in a town with a largely uneducated agricultural workforce to a town that hosts some of the world's best minds in the fields of physics, chemistry, engineering and bioscience. But if we take the arrival of the Metropolitan Railway as the advent of modern Amersham, that transformation in the world of work has taken just 125 years.

Medical isotopes were carried around the world in wing tip compartments in the 1960s.

Today GE Healthcare manufacture a range of MRI scanners and imaging devices.

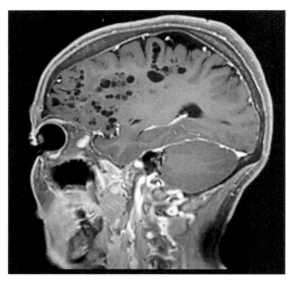

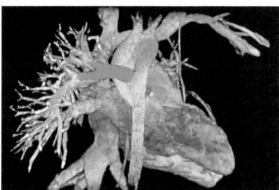

Above, left, below, opposite above:
Advanced visualisation combines
technologies to give clinicians
stunningly detailed images of the
human body.

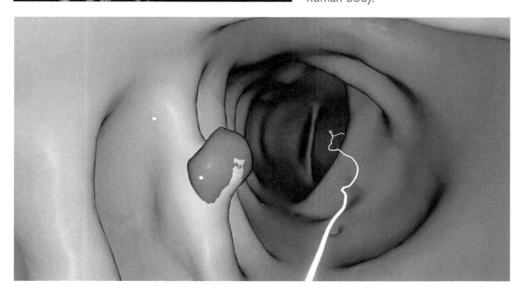

Senographe Pristina is a system that allows women to take control of the mammography process.

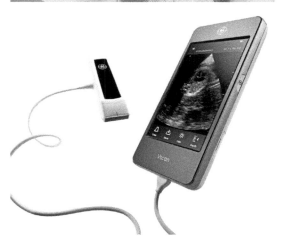

Vscan is a portable mini-ultrasound unit.

ACKNOWLEDGEMENTS

I am most grateful to Emily Toettcher, the curator of the Amersham Museum, for her invaluable help and guidance in the research for this book, and also for her permission to use the museum's archive of photography and the many online articles written by members of the Amersham Society and archived at the museum.

My thanks also go to John Clutterbuck, who gave me many useful contacts and generously gave me his time to explain the roles of the principal Amersham families engaged in the town's businesses and industries. John's comments on the draft text also removed some inconsistencies.

Roy Miller and Peter Clark provided me with useful information about the development of railways in the Amersham area and also about the Amersham Home Guard in the Second World War.

Julian Hunt's 2001 book *A History of Amersham* is the definitive contemporary work on the town's history. It gave me the wider background to the stories of enterprise and work that make up the subject of this book.

Other helpful reading has included *The Story of John Brazil* as told to and written by Jean Archer and lent to me by the museum. Also *The Penn Country of Buckinghamshire* published in 1932 by the Council for the Preservation of Rural England.

For accounts of present-day businesses in Amersham I am indebted to Hanna Huntley of GE Healthcare, Gary Grant of The Entertainer, and Kevin Fox of Fox's Limited.

I would also like to thank the following for providing photographs and giving permission for their use: Amersham Museum, Gary Grant, GE Healthcare, Peter Clark and Kevin Fox. All images are © Amersham Museum unless stated otherwise.

Amersham is fortunate to possess a vast online historical archive that has been indispensable in the writing of this book, and anyone interested in the town's history will find a wealth of further information at www.amershamhistory.info.

William Parker
Great Kimble, 2017